Brother John
The Monk Who Made Everyone Smile

Copyright © 2025 by Isaac Slater

ISBN: 978-1-945423-77-2

Artwork by Christopher Tupa
ctupa.com / christophertupa@hotmail.com

All rights reserved. No part of this publication may be reproduced, distributed, or transmitted in any form or by any means, including photocopying, recording, or other electronic or mechanical methods, without the prior written permission of the publisher, except in the case of brief quotations embodied in critical reviews and certain other noncommercial uses permitted by copyright law.
For permission requests, write to the publisher at the address below.

5 Stones Publishing
Fairport NY, 14450
Randy2905@gmail.com

Once there was a monk named Brother John who really loved people. He also loved to drive fast! When he was young he got in some trouble, but when he was old, even though he was often sick, he made everyone who met him smile.

Before he became a monk he played violin for the local orchestra.

He also loved to race cars.

He learned to write in beautiful calligraphy and would often copy out the psalms as a way to pray. He would memorize his favorite psalms as well.

He also played his violin in a quartet with other monks when the psalms were sung in church. He loved to use his gift for music as a way to praise God.

Once when he had finally found a monastery where he felt at home but was still having trouble settling in, he was asked to work in the garage. He was a great mechanic. He also met more people at the garage and this helped him a lot. He really loved people and before long he was making them smile.

Brother John kept praying the Psalms. He sang them in choir with the other monks, wrote them out in his beautiful calligraphy, and continued to learn his favorite psalms by heart. Over time, as he grew closer to God in prayer, he became very peaceful. His natural love for people became even deeper and more wholehearted.

When he wasn't working on cars Brother John fixed machines in the bakery. One time a monk got his arm caught in a giant bread molder.

Father Josaphat, who was an engineer, went off to find the right sized screw-diver to carefully take apart the molder.

J.B. grabbed a giant crow-bar and pried the rollers on the molder right open!

Once as a younger monk he was driving a visiting bishop and several abbots to a meeting. He was stuck behind a car that was going VERY slow and he was getting more and more impatient... while the abbots and the bishops talked on and on...

Suddenly he sped up swerved onto the steep grass median, shot past the car and zipped off down the road!

As much as he loved to go fast JB came to love being still even more. Even when he was quite old himself he often helped care for monks who were older or very sick. One monk who was 99 years old was often anxious. JB would sit with him quietly, eyes closed, and before long the ancient monk would grow calm.

When he grew old Brother John was often sick.
Sometimes there were emergencies and Father Jed
would have to race him to the hospital in the
middle of the night.
No matter how badly he felt, J.B. would always perk up
as Father Jed drove faster and faster!

It was during his stays in hospital toward the end of his life that Brother John really made everyone smile. Even though he was so weak, he quickly learned the names of all the nurses and aides. They would come to visit him on their breaks, tell him their stories, and talk about their problems.

Father Jed was often with Brother John in hospital. To pass the time, and to make him smile, Brother John would teach him the sign language the older monks had used. The signs were pretty simple but J.B. and the others would combine them in funny ways to make each other laugh.

Father Jed would remember these new and improved signs and use them back at the monastery to surprise the older monks!

One time after a stay in hospital Father Jed was wheeling him down the hall and the head nurse ran after them...she gave Brother John a big hug. She was sad to see him go, and even crying, but only because he had made her smile so often.

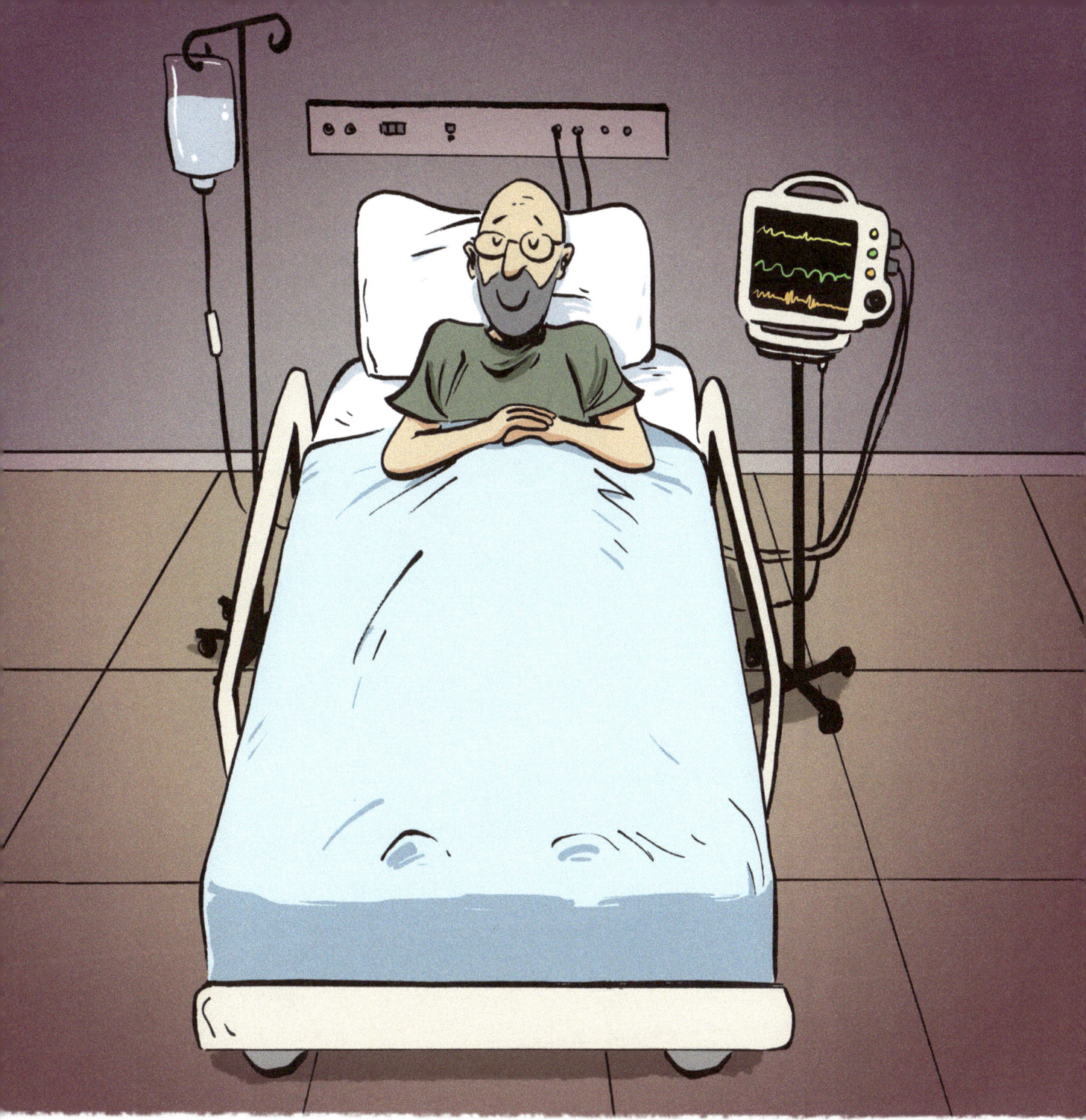

When he was alone he would draw near to God in his heart and pray the many psalms he had memorized throughout his life. He knew that he was loved, all the way down, and he let this love flow through him to everyone he met.

The Lord is my light and my help;
whom shall I fear?
The Lord is the stronghold of my life;
before whom shall I shrink?

There is one thing I ask of the Lord,
for this I long.
To live in the house of the Lord,
all the days of my life.
To savor the sweetness
    of the Lord,
to behold his temple.